HYMN DUETS

CONTENTS

— PIANO LEVEL —
LATE INTERMEDIATE/EARLY ADVANCED

ISBN 978-1-4234-3696-6

HAL•LEONARD®
CORPORATION
7777 W. BLUEMOUND RD. P.O. BOX 13819 MILWAUKEE, WI 53213

In Australia Contact:
Hal Leonard Australia Pty. Ltd.
4 Lentara Court
Cheltenham, Victoria, 3192 Australia
Email: ausadmin@halleonard.com.au

Visit Hal Leonard Online at
www.halleonard.com

Visit Phillip at
www.phillipkeveren.com

PREFACE

Duets are fun. The typical practice routine for the pianist is rather solitary, so rehearsing with another musician is a welcome change of pace. If two heads are better than one, then surely four hands and twenty fingers have to be great!

Hymns provide a wealth of inspiring musical material. The titles in this collection are some of my personal favorites. I have grouped some of them topically to create medleys. I hope you will reference the hymn text of any one of these with which you may be unfamiliar. This will certainly help to inform your interpretation of the arrangement.

Sincerely,
Phillip Keveren

BIOGRAPHY

Phillip Keveren, a multi-talented keyboard artist and composer, has composed original works in a variety of genres from piano solo to symphonic orchestra. Mr. Keveren gives frequent concerts and workshops for teachers and their students in the United States, Canada, Europe, and Asia. Mr. Keveren holds a B.M. in composition from California State University Northridge and a M.M. in composition from the University of Southern California.

HYMNS OF ADORATION

Arranged by Phillip Keveren

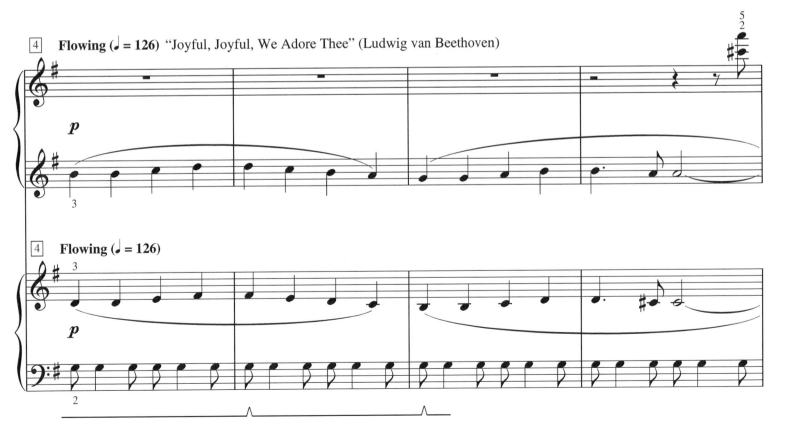

Reverently ($\quarternote$ = 76) "Fairest Lord Jesus" (Silesian Folk Melody)

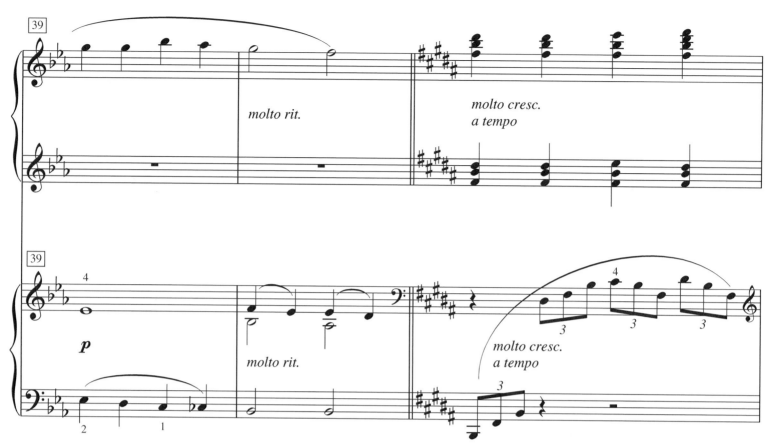

Triumphantly (♩ = 84) "All Hail the Power of Jesus' Name" (Oliver Holden)

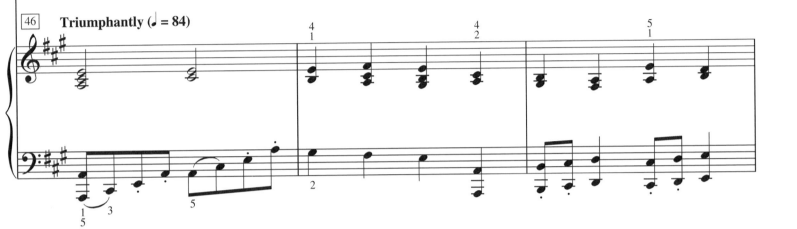

ALL CREATURES OF OUR GOD AND KING

Words by FRANCIS OF ASSISI
Translated by WILLIAM HENRY DRAPER
Music from *Geistliche Kirchengesang*
Arranged by Phillip Keveren

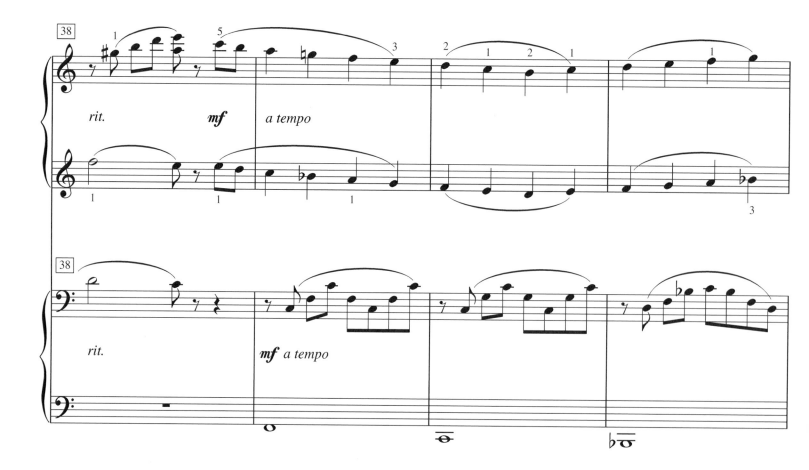

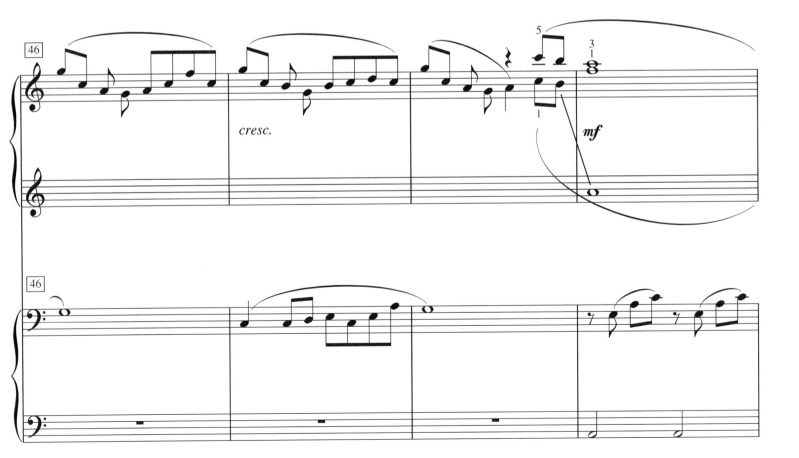

HYMNS OF MAJESTY

Arranged by Phillip Keveren

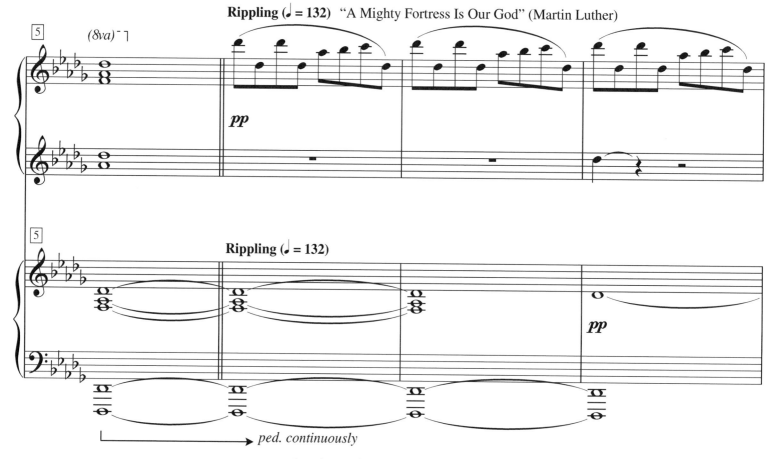

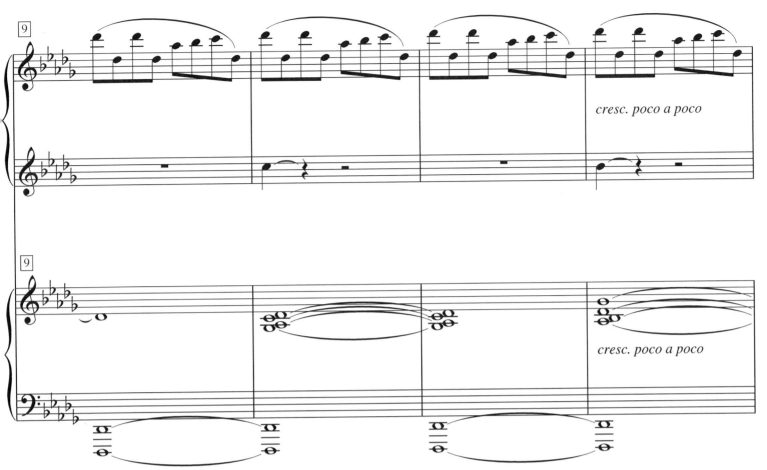

"Holy, Holy, Holy!" (John B. Dykes)

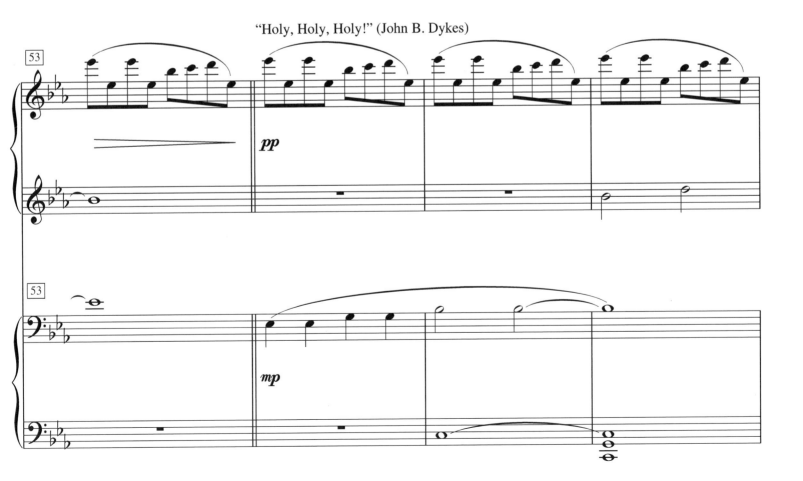

Stately (♩ = **104**)   "Immortal, Invisible" (Traditional Welsh Melody)

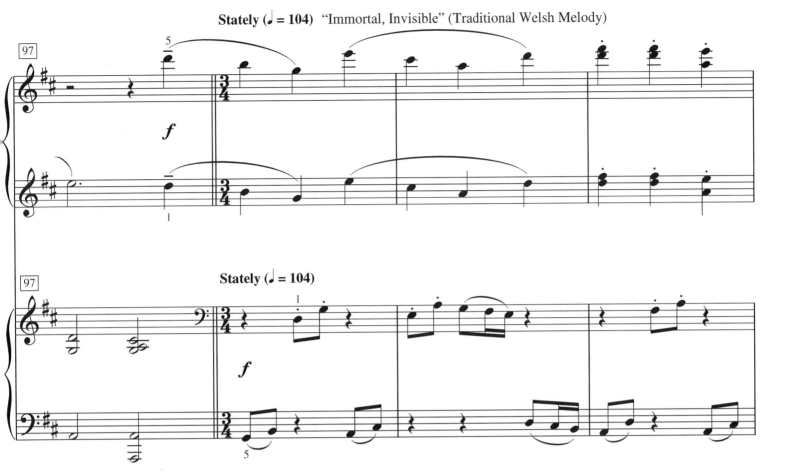

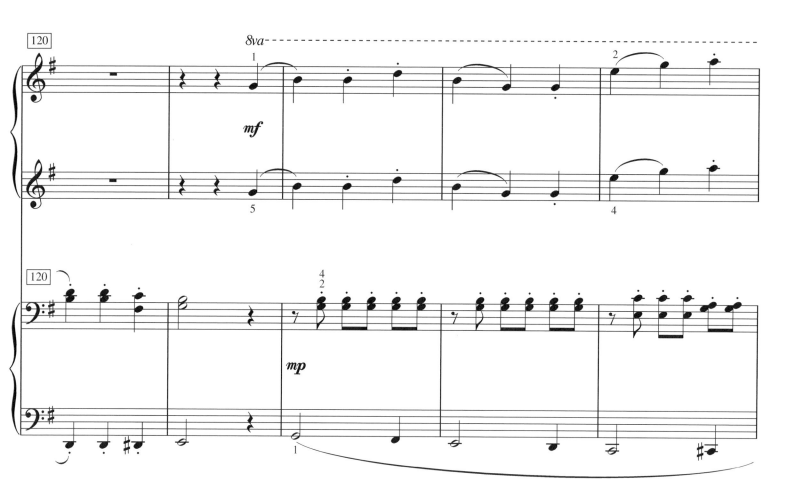

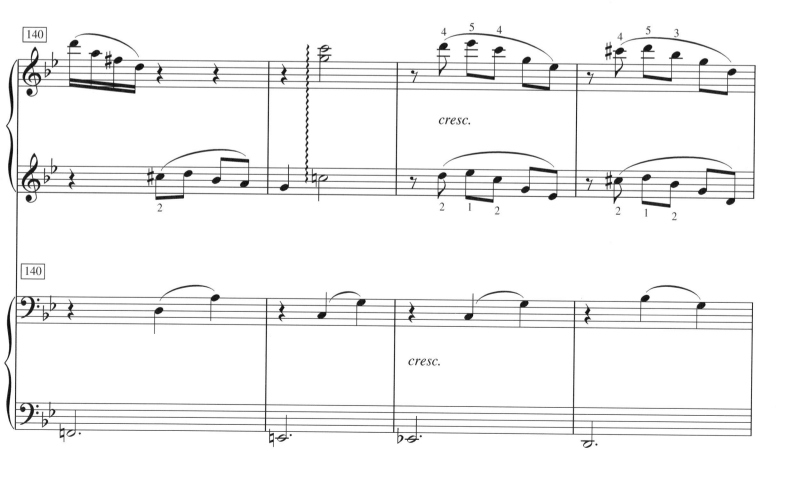

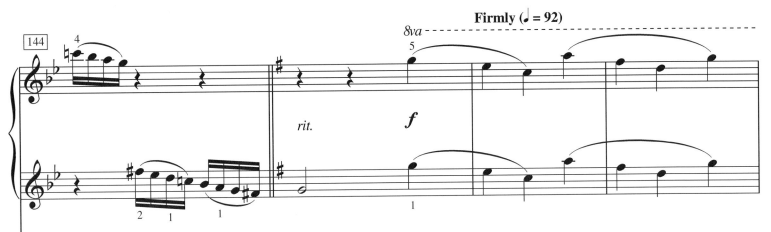

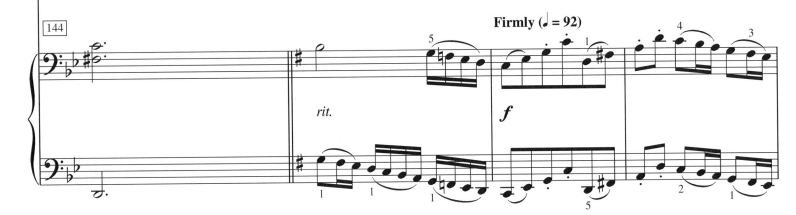

I SURRENDER ALL

Words by J.W. VAN DEVENTER
Music by W.S. WEEDEN
Arranged by Phillip Keveren

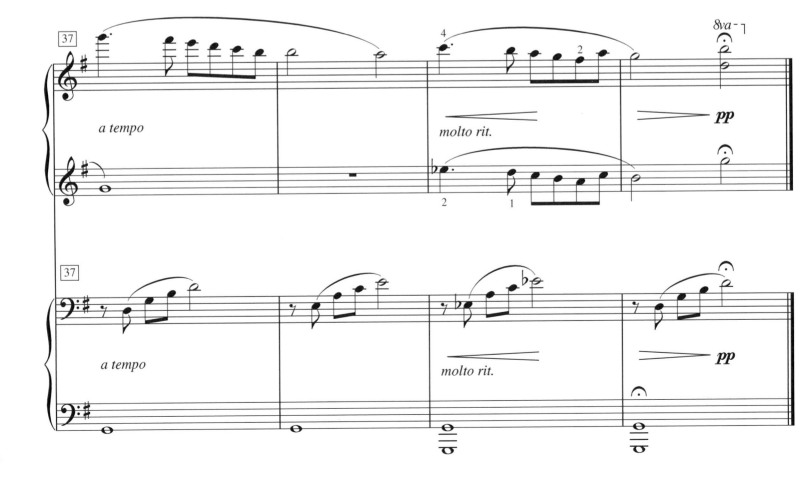

IT IS WELL WITH MY SOUL

Words by HORATIO G. SPAFFORD
Music by PHILIP P. BLISS
Arranged by Phillip Keveren

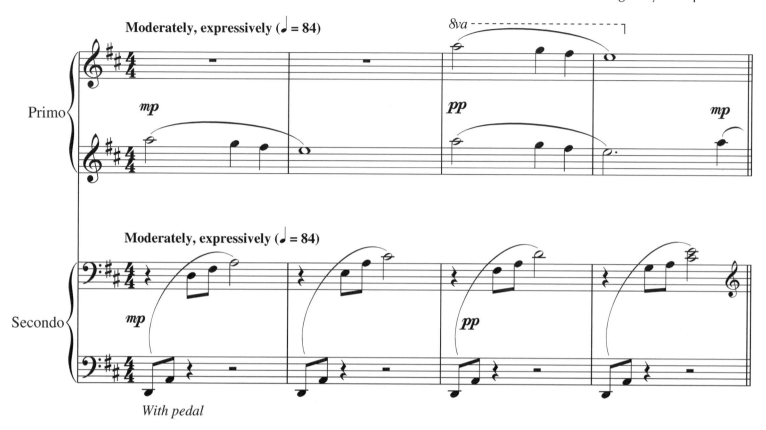

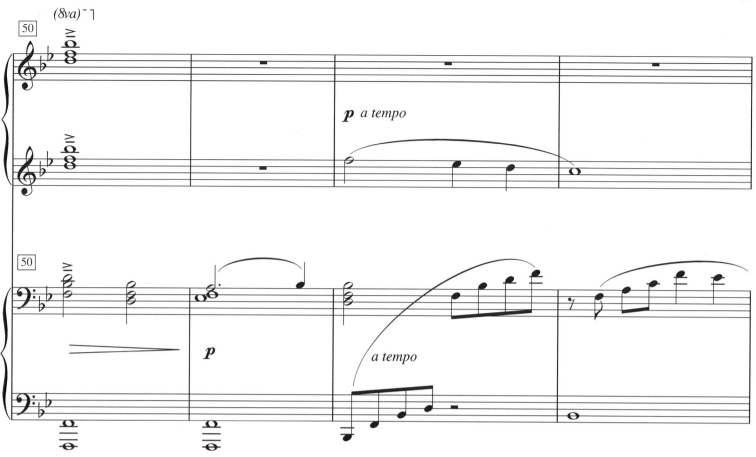

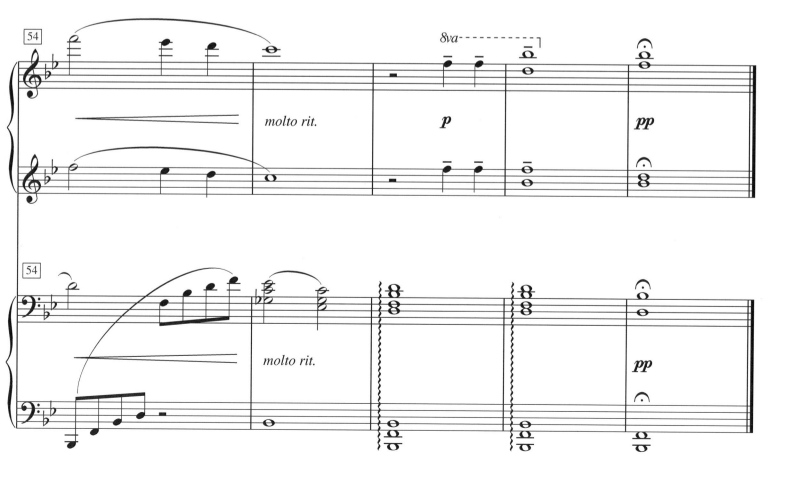

O SACRED HEAD, NOW WOUNDED

Words by BERNARD OF CLAIRVAUX
Music by HANS LEO HASSLER
Arranged by Phillip Keveren

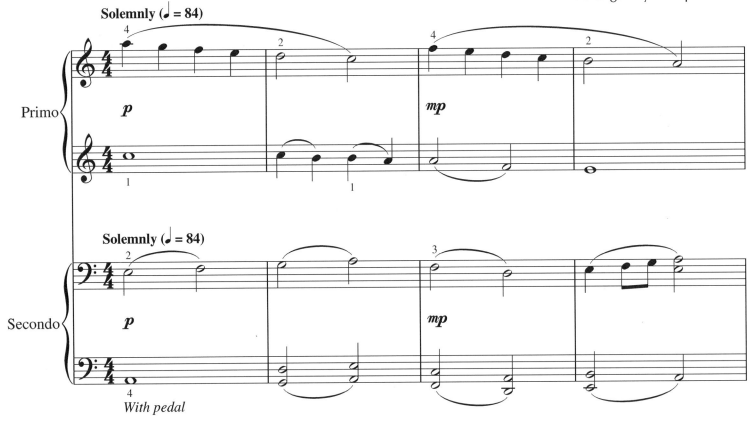

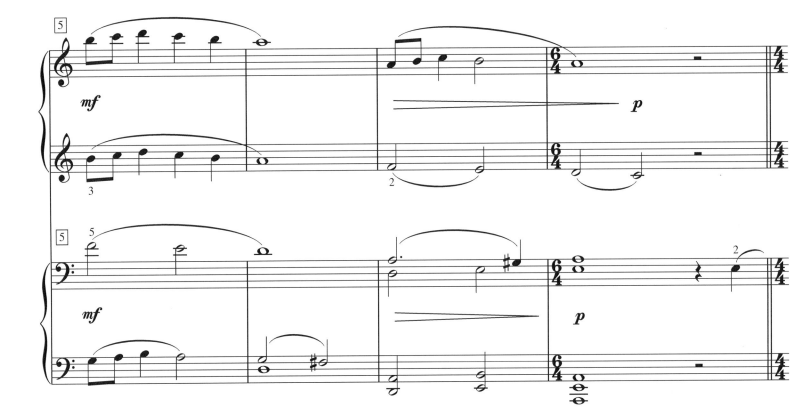

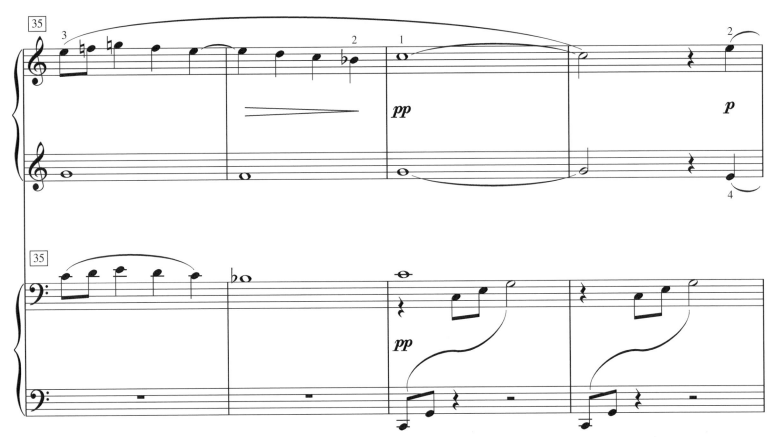

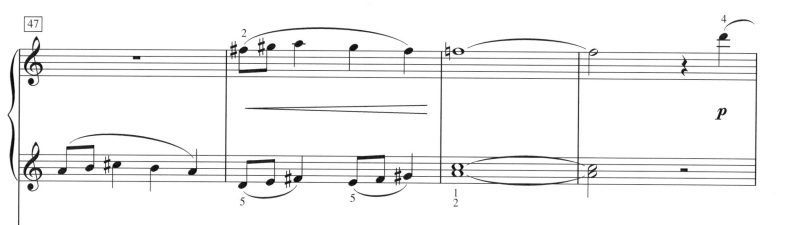

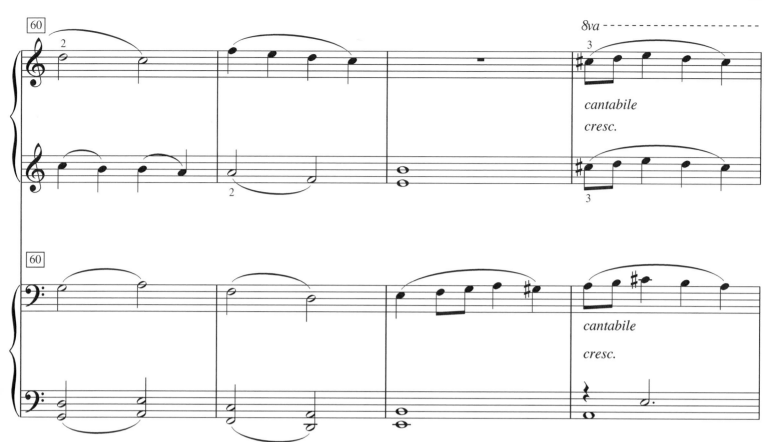

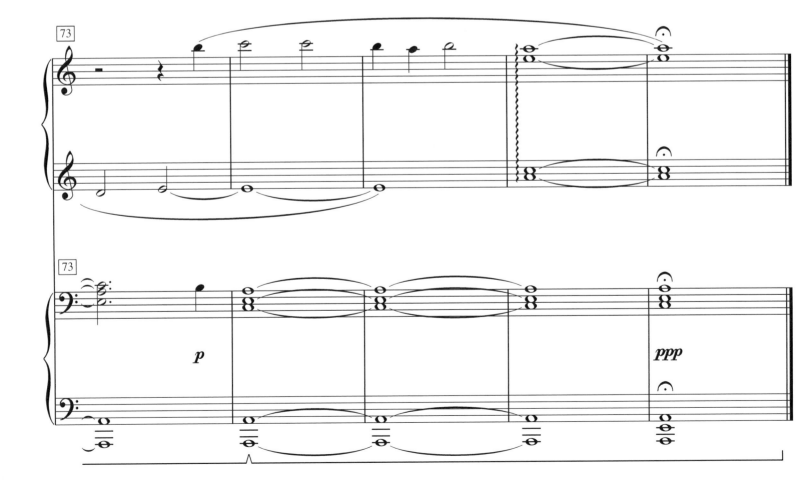

PRAISE TO THE LORD, THE ALMIGHTY

Words by JOACHIM NEANDER
Translated by CATHERINE WINKWORTH
Music from *Erneuerten Gesangbuch*
Arranged by Phillip Keveren

64

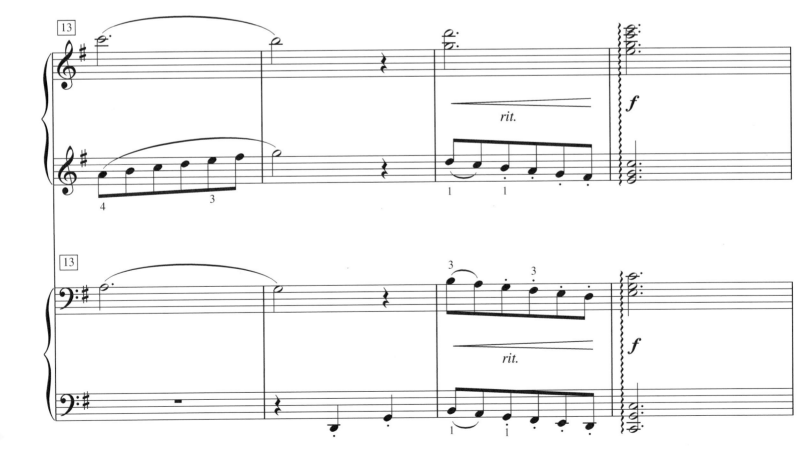

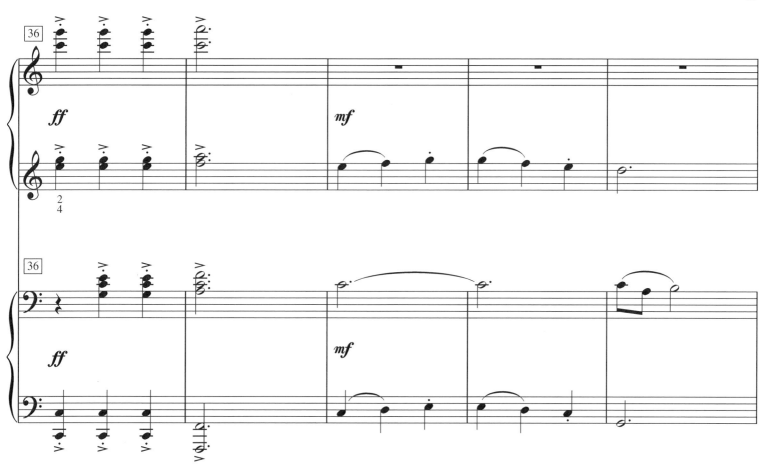

REJOICE, THE LORD IS KING

Words by CHARLES WESLEY
Music by JOHN DARWALL
Arranged by Phillip Keveren